# I am

**Pheobe  Mcmahon.**

BookLeaf
Publishing

India | USA | UK

Presentation by *BookLeaf Publishing*

Web: www.bookleafpub.com

E-mail: info@bookleafpub.com

ISBN: 9789357213813

First edition 2022

# ACKNOWLEDGEMENT

Writing poetry is so much harder than I first anticipated, none of this would've been possible without my best friend, Ellie. She was the first person who truly saw me and helped me to create ideas for my writing.

I'm eternally grateful to my high school English teacher, who really helped me understand my passion for writing and further encouraged me to pursue in a literacy future.

Finally I would like to thank my mum, who made all of this possible. Without her love and support I never would've been able to publish a book, she has encouraged me to keep writing and helped me get through a time of my life when I was struggling.

# PREFACE

A couple of years ago I was struggling with anxiety and coming to terms with my sexuality, so I decided to start writing poetry as a way to express the feelings I thought I couldn't share with anyone.

But here I am, sharing my thoughts with you.

# desperate to be heard.

Oh, I love to be alone
at peace with myself.
listening to music by myself
brings an odd array of comfort.

Sitting in my room,
the smell of freshly lit candles
with a book of conversed words
which hold such an odd impact over me.

Oh, I hate being lonely.
feeling an emptiness in myself
trying to fill a void by myself
brings an odd array of despondency.

Sitting in my room,
soothing myself in silence with
Murmuring laughter screaming down my ears
which make me feel so empty.

Oh, being alone is like a feeling of
independence,
It makes you feel comfort from having a place
where you feel at one with your being.

But being lonely is like being submerged under
clear water
Watching everybody else have the life you yearn
and yet no body can hear your pleas and begs

Because you're lonely.

# the nobody.

It's like they can see right through me,
like I'm simply not there
unless it's convenient for them to see me,
I'm simply a transparent body lingering around
the crowded town.

I'm a good friend only for the comforts I offer,
never for being me.
and when they no longer need me,
I once again dissolve into the segments of the
earth.

It's not even like I'm a person anymore.

Maybe if I got their attention
I would be able to confabulate my own words,
instead of just listening to theirs.

Maybe if I smiled more, they'd smile back,
just like how they do at each other.

My friends simply do not care.
to them, I'm nothing more than a tissue.
to be used once then thrown away
like I'm nothing.

My supposedly real body is like air
that simply fades when my friends turn their
back once again
allowing them to not notice the blank space

A blank space where the nobody lingers.

# in love

The hardest thing I've had to come to acceptance
with is being in love with you.

Even now simply knowing that I'm infatuated
with your whole being daunts me because I
know it's wrong.

It's so wrong, like it was never meant to be, me
and you. We are simply two souls never destined
to cross scattered paths and yet we did anyway.

And now I feel pink dust dispersing along my
cheeks when the thought of you crosses my
mind

Is two girls loving each other really so
disgusting?
even though I may not know the correct answer I
cannot stop devoting myself to you.

It's all the diminutive qualities about your being
that make me fall for you a bit more each time,
and my love for you is now eternal.

I didn't think I knew what love was until I met
you,

And I'm willing to sacrifice people's idea of
society if it means our souls can be one, because
perhaps I have been been blinded by love or I
plainly just love you.

# a flower

Flowers grow from within me, from my mouth
down to my feet.
I can't do anything except see,
see myself for the things I have become, what
I've transformed into.

"You're beautiful" Society reassured me, with
the same flowers of false pretence growing
through them,
But how far did I have to go
to be deemed
beautiful?

My mind pictures the artist brutally piercing
holes through my lungs, planting flowers
through my eyes and mouth
so when people find me,
they will see the beauty.

Take the focus away from the fact
I'm internally bleeding from the punctured lungs

And to be frank, society is the culprit
It gave me the seeds to plant the flamboyance of
the flowers-

exactly the same as everyone else's.

But to be frank, I did this to myself,
I took the seeds without caring for the
consequences

Because I gave too much power to the flowers
that once captivated me with their virtue, I have
into the voices telling me to quench their thirst
and rid them of their sorrow
But were they to blame
How far did I have to go to be deemed
Beautiful?

Must I really carve out my face and put seeds
through my body?
have my insides scuttle and scratch themselves
apart to be an average standard to people?
How far did I have to go to be deemed
Normal?

# to be nothing or everything

"I'm so proud of you"
The compliments used to flow through her ears
like a melody.
"gifted and talented" and "highest in the class"
they'd praise with blinding smiles
They all expected so highly of me, but as long as
they payed her some attention right?

"i'm so proud of you"
The compliments no longer feel so rewarding, as
the teacher now tells that to everyone.
she must have burnt out the talent and gifted
traits that lingered within her because now she's
simply average
With nobody sparing her a single glance.

Is this all she is now?
Simply nothing. Without her achieving grades
she bas nothing to make people swoon over her.
she's just a figure that is now the same as
everybody else

But she doesn't want that.
She cant be nothing. She can't have worked so
hard for so long just to have the same chances as

the people who don't try, she wants to be the one
teachers are proud of.

She wont accept being a nothing,
And that's ultimately her harmarta- to be nothing
or everything
And in this case, she would chose everything,
every time
Even if it kills her.

# a star

From the young adolescence
She would always put the culminate touches
onto the tree
A star.
Just how her parents described her, a star.
She would receive a golden star from her
teachers to say "you done well" and it was stuck
on her bedroom wall,  her parents took her out to
celebrate.
They'd go out laughing and dancing like the
stereotypical family,
So maybe they were. Maybe they were the
happy family that spent every doting minute
together
But they all loved each other and that's what
mattered.
She'd ask her parents if she would ever fall in
love like how they did, they'd laugh to each
other with a layer of ardour coating their eyes
before tucking the young child into bed.
They'd always tuck her into bed.

Two years later they had split up,
Not quite a divorce but enough to stop seeing
each other

She had woke up to a smash and her parents
yelling to each other and it was in that moment
that any longing she had to fall in love had
shattered as she watched her parents slowly fall
apart like a star dying in the monochromatic sky.
She never did truly understand then, the concept
of what had happened. And yet the only
memory's she had with the happy family were
the ones in old photographs stored under the
rustic bed.
But she still tried to see both of her parents.
The girl would still receive golden stars, not as
often but enough to say she was still working
amazingly.
Her walls still hadn't lost their shine as more
stickers got added to the wallpaper.
And yet her parents never tucked her in anymore
And she cried for them to do it again
          Like how they used to.

The girl no longer received the stars,
She was "too mature", "too old" for them now
her old stickers started too disintegrate just like
her fascination with falling in love.
and it was then she finally knew, she was never
destined to have the same love that her parents
once had.

That's why on the back of her old photos she
tried to confabulate how she felt, she wrote a
poem
And said she called it "a star"
And then she sobbed some more and
Sliced a tear on each wrist
Then simply hung it on the bathroom door
Because this time she couldn't reach the stars
        Not like how she was destined too.
She was no longer tall enough to put the star on
the tree as her body simply fell like the stars
falling down.

# nor life or death.

In both birth and death, we are inevitable.

To be aware of the discernment that our beings
endure,
to be emanated into the fragments we call life,
just too slowly hear the abating beats of our
dying hearts.

I desire however, to simply forgot about the
realisation that we are truly dying.
our fate is a concept in which literature cannot
predict
and that, is the most formidable thought we can
think.

I want to live.
I want to live without mourning to this array of
mortality that clings to our beings in a grasp so
tight it burns.

I want to live as though this life amounts to
nothing but more.
To be sentient for an eternity is pushing my
being further into the pit of morbid mourning
As I realise, I am bound to die.

We all are.

Life is simply baiting us,
And we cannot do anything except wait,
Longing to feel the solace of our beings
Before the sting of death seeps in
And our bodies once again become nothing
more
than fragments of the earth.

# eternally on cobble.

Is it simply that the once green fields have
eroded or have I simply been walking on sharp
cobble since my first gait?

My feet start to become crimson as each rustic
stone digs once more into my skin.
Every time I try to pick out the pieces- I realise
that it's simply exorbitant.

To go back would cause as much blood to flow
as carrying on would give. All I can do is feel
the surroundings and further burn my skin.

My mind yearns to picture the virescence fields
and yet as I sprint towards the nourished floors
It simply slips from my grasps and my soles are
left with gashes soaking up the gore that my
being tried to fight.

Even to try and leave my trail of blood,
show how hard i'm fighting against the stone,
It would be pointless
As nobody ever noticed the fact there was
crimson soaking on me anyway
simply because it isn't discernible.

And in the end,
the road ahead of me is so lonely,
as the cobble prevails over every piece of skin i
have left
until i will no longer be able to walk.

Then i will rigorously sink into the cobble that
caused my ultimate suffering.

# the snowman.

You picked up my once broken pieces
And embossed them back together with
A lot of endearment and solicitude
To fix the once shattered pieces of my being.

You even gave me more features
to make me feel more welcomed.
With love, you gifted me a hat
And wrapped me in a scarf to keep
My once haemorrhage wounds
Sealed by the puce scarf you placed on me.

It stayed like this for a while,
Just me and you.
Living in the small junctures that made
Smiles melt on both our faces.

As the glaciers started to melt
So did the amount of affection you gave me.
The warmth you once gave me started to droop
And the frigidness of the once consoling floors
Started to disintegrate as did my body.

Yet your eyes still never bore into mine anymore
As I watch you stay inside all day round

Did the iciness that permeate through me drive
you away?
Im not surprised, it always does.

The longer you left me, the quicker my body
seemed to melt
Because how could I live without knowing that
you cared about me?
But at least you're merry inside the confinements
of the warmth.

At least one of us could make it to the comfort.

# Falling into the past.

I want to live every day.
Be perennial in every moment
But my thoughts remain adhered in yesterday.
And although my feet are glued in today
My mind traces fastidiously around the scars of
yesterday

My body and mind cannot conspire together
As my being is torn between 2 different places.
So, it artlessly is torn between them.
The concept of then and now

The past is a concept of self-reflection
Which I know I shouldn't mourn upon.
Yet I find myself pensively dreaming about what
could've been
rather than what has.

So, to live in such a place with our desires
Is merely a concept which humans yearn to
endure
And if we ever do grasp onto an opportunity in
this lifetime
It often disappears into an emptiness.

As does our infatuation with living in the
present.

21

# believing thoughtlessness is a crime.

I wish that my thoughts took up more space
within my brain
Instead of feeling this vacant and futile thing
I can no longer call my mind.

My thoughts itch to have some purpose
but whenever I try to conjure any sort of
emotion or memory
It simply permeates into emptiness

And the only thing I am left with
desolation pulsing through my veins
and an overwhelming emotion of
nothing.

Nothingness- it almost feels like a crime
to have such little care about things that matter
to not care about the thoughts that should flow
through my head
and with that, it could be said that my
thoughtlessness is a destined crime for my mind.

# poisonous.

Your heart ruptured in the venom of my words
as they grovelled into your self worth.

I didn't know, I didn't know I would break your
innocence
and carve cuts through every piece of kindness
you had left.

My gut knows it was my fault, I said those
things
and yet my mind keeps giving me fake
reassurance
that it wasn't.

the pieces of your soul revolted
and yet I was still so blinded with narcissism to
see
the poison running through your veins.

As I didn't want to accept my colossal aspect
in your emotional demise
but it has always been my fault and I deduce that
it's finally time I accepted that.

I'm sorry, I'm sorry for forcing my lies down
your throat
My mind squeezes every living memory as I
realise, I made the poison to fill your thoughts.

I created your poison and I'm eternally sorry.

# better off solitary.

Every day, the phone rings.
but I don't answer it, I never answer it
call back tonight, or maybe tomorrow or even
never

I crawl back into that eternal pit of grief and
turmoil
"you're just self-inflicting pain onto yourself"
 my therapist once told me.

So yes, maybe I do cause myself this internal
misery
cradling myself in the veil of the night.
I am the one who threw myself into this
gloaming place,

Craving solitude, to simply be alone
and disregard every upcoming implication that
permeates through my meaningless journey.

And in moments like that,
seclusion is a necessary trait that lingers within
me
as I crawl back into isolation-away from others.

The one place where I can truly see myself
as clear as fresh water
except I'm not fresh.

My being further sinks into the morbid
lonesomeness
yet the only thing I can see through this water
is every single flaw I obtain.

So, here my soul lies in this isolation
drowning inside this pit of emptiness, alone
from everybody
but at least this is where I truly know myself.

# just a piece of normality.

This world has chewed me up and spat me out
before I had even fully understood the concept
of life
It grimaced at my young imagination
before driving it all away leaving me with
insipidity.

It didn't know that I was just a sweet child,
full of innocence and complex ideas
and yet it simply did not care.

I watched it strip away every pure and gentle
quality
Before replacing it with harsh and malicious
intent
And admiring the work it had produced with me
Before sending me back down into the earth
hopeless.

It simply chewed on my bones and drank my
blood
Like a cuisine, a hobby to watch me turn
imitative
Just like everybody else.

This world consumed every drop of diversity I
had
Before leaving me stranded in the place you call
"comfort"
and leaving me in the never-ending cycle of
humanities judgement
with no traits to make me aberrant.

# forever mourning.

Please
Come back.
Even as a shadow,
Even as a ghost.

Haunt my sleep again, let me picture your face
again
Trace my fingers along your sculpted features
Don't let me forget you,
Allow me to grasp onto you and wish you were
still here.

Haunt my thoughts again, consume every fibre
in my being
And don't let me heal from our perishing
memories
Don't let me forget you,
Let me cry and mourn over your absence once
more.

Haunt my whole life, let me give you my whole
heart
Then never give it back so I always have a
reason to be with you
Don't let me forget you,

Even if it costs my life, I will eternally mourn
you
        My love.

vulnerable against your
words.


You somehow found out I was gay before I did
Did you see that as some sort of advantage?
to know one of the impure things about me
before I understood myself
did it feel good to finally figure out the reason I
didn't like boys with idealistic bodies?
Well congratulations.

Congratulations, you told my peers before I
could even breathe
as this harsh reality keeps forcing me into the
water of morality.
I trusted you and you walked away,
giving me no comfort or reassurance as you
vamoose out of my life.

But, hey, at least you told them for me, initially
you set me free
You took the initiative and told people what I
knew I couldn't.

However, the part that hurt the most was when I
never knew.

You betrayed me and the fact never grasped until
a year later
when I had gathered up the courage to tell them,
their eyes glistened with confusion like they
knew something I didn't
they knew about me- about who I am.

So well done, you told everybody
and I truly hope you feel proud of yourself for
making me feel so enclosed.
I hope that my sexuality made you feel that burst
of pride you have always wanted, even though
you must have wanted that more than our
friendship.

in my November solitude.

A chill found its way down my neck
Winter is falling down upon me
I step outside at twilight
the snow glistens on my fingertips
the cold air bites against my flustered cheeks

This is the dawning reminder
That November has come around once more
Along side the frosty emotions that ensues
within
The eery month of solitude.

# yearning to be a teen.

"You lived your best life" people tell me
as I sit in a good college with outstanding
grades.
But would you describe that as my "best" life?

My entire teenage experience was studying to
try and be the best person I could be, to try being
top of my classes and get the best academic
offers.

And yet as I reflect on those years I am filled
with rue
I wish I was a teen title
living the normal teenage dream, trying to fit
society's standards

I've never known what it feels like to go out
drinking on weekends
or go shopping and compare outfits.
simply because my mind was so fixated on
being the best.

My being is eternally grateful for giving it the
greatest options

However, if I could go back and try to endure
some aspects of the idealistic experience
          Then I would.

And I would try to be 'normal', have a large
group of friends
but unfortunately, I didn't do that, I put my
academics first
so, I might be better off now but at what cost?

What did I lose out on for the letter 'A' on a
piece of paper?

www.ingramcontent.com/pod-product-compliance
Lightning Source LLC
LaVergne TN
LVHW051240200726

843510LV00011B/1625